SEASONS SEASONS SEASONS SEASONS

SUMMER

Moira Butterfield

Illustrated by Helen James

A⁺

Smart Apple Media

Published by Smart Apple Media
2140 Howard Drive West, North Mankato, MN 56003

Designed and illustrated by Helen James

Photographs by Corbis (Asian Art & Archaeology, Paul Barton, Ray Bird;
Frank Lane Picture Agency, E.O. Hoppé, Rob Howard, Martin Jones, Wolfgang
Kaehler, George D. Lepp, Chris Lisle, Robert Llewelyn, Buddy Mays, Ariel Skelley)

Printed and bound in Thailand

Library of Congress Cataloging-in-Publication Data

Butterfield, Moira.
Summer / by Moira Butterfield.
p. cm. — (Seasons)
Includes index.
ISBN 1-58340-615-8
1. Summer—Juvenile literature. I. Title.

QB637.6.B88 2005
508.2—dc22   2005042576

First Edition

9 8 7 6 5 4 3 2 1

Contents

All about summer

Summer is a season, a time of year when the weather is warm. Most people love summer!

The sun gives us life. Without it, there would be no animals or plants on our planet.

Our sizzling sun
We get warmth and light from the sun.
It is a huge, fiery ball of burning gas.
Earth travels around the sun.
It takes one year to go all the
way around.

Earth words
The two halves of Earth are called the northern and southern hemispheres. While one has summer, the other has winter. The area around the middle of Earth is called the equator.

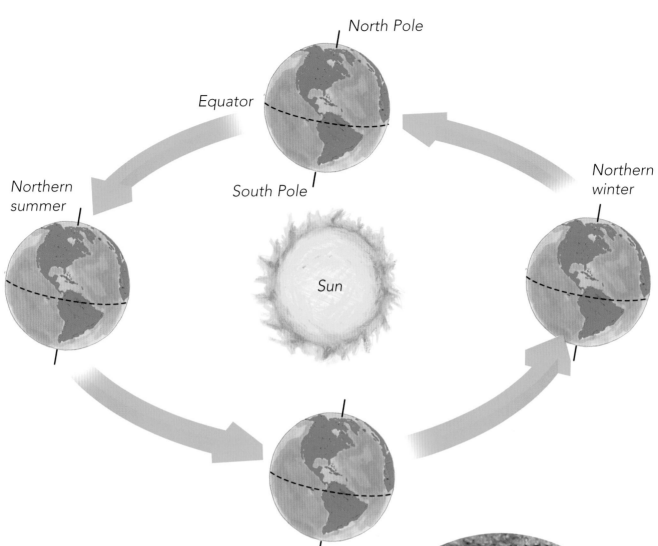

North Pole

Equator

South Pole

Northern summer

Northern winter

Sun

Summer or winter?

Earth leans toward the sun as it travels around it. The half closest to the sun has summer, and the other half has winter. So, as Earth gradually turns around, the seasons change.

Poles stay cold

The areas at the far north and south of Earth are called poles. They are never close enough to the sun to get really hot in the summer. They are always covered in ice.

My summer, your summer

Summer does not come at the same time for everyone. When it is summer for you, it is winter on the other side of the world.

Summer north and south

In Earth's northern half, summer comes in June, July, and August. In Earth's southern half, summer comes in December, January, and February.

What about the middle?

In countries along the equator, it is hot year-round. There is no winter or summer. Places near the equator have wet and dry seasons instead.

Days and nights

As Earth travels around the sun, it spins in space like a top. It takes 24 hours to spin once. First one side faces the sun, then the other, giving us days and nights. In the summer, days are longer and nights are shorter.

The hottest summer place in the northern hemisphere is the Sahara Desert in North Africa.

The equator has wet and dry seasons.

The hottest summer place in the southern hemisphere is Queensland, Australia.

Sun at bedtime

In the far north of the world, called the Arctic, the summer sun shines all day and all night. That is why it is called the "land of the midnight sun." Around the top of the world, the Arctic sea freezes in the winter and melts in the summer. But the North Pole always stays frozen.

Summer snow

The far south of the world is called Antarctica. In the summer, the sun shines day and night but never melts the snow. The sun's rays bounce off the snow and are so dazzling that visitors have to wear sunglasses, even though they are dressed warmly.

The summer sun shines at midnight near the North Pole.

Summer's coming

When summer comes, the weather grows warmer and the days last longer. There is more time to play outside! Watch for these summer signs.

What's buzzing?

Insects hatch in warm weather. You'll know summer is coming when you spot a butterfly or hear a buzzing bee. You might even get an itchy bite on your skin from a summer insect called a mosquito.

What's croaking?

Frogs and toads call to each other. They come out at night, when the air is cooler. Crickets signal to each other by rubbing their wings together.

Can you feel summer?

You can feel summer coming because the temperature rises outside. We measure temperature with a thermometer that has a colored liquid inside it. The liquid squeezes up a thin tube as it gets warmer. Numbers along the tube measure how far up the liquid goes.

These numbers show the temperature, measured in degrees Fahrenheit (°F) or degrees Celsius (°C).

Can you see summer?

Sometimes you look into the distance and see that the air seems to be wobbling. This happens when the weather is hot and heat rises up from the ground.

Can you touch summer?

The summer sun heats up objects. Have you noticed how hot the seats in your car can be in summer? Touch them to feel some of the sun's power!

Summer and you

The temperature of the sun is hotter than the warmest oven or the fiercest fire. That's why you can feel its warmth even though it is 93 million miles (150 million km) away.

Water out, water in

Your skin has lots of tiny holes in it, called pores. When you get warm, water comes out of your body through your pores. The water evaporates, which means it disappears into the air. This helps to cool you down by taking some of your body heat away with it.

Slip on some shades

Strong summer sunlight can hurt your eyes, so you need sunglasses to shield them from the glare. Never look directly at the sun, even with sunglasses on. Its light is so strong it would damage your eyes forever.

In warm weather, you need to drink lots of water to replace the water you lose through your pores.

Skin and sun

Skin has a substance called melanin inside it that helps protect it from being burned by the sun. People with light skin have less melanin than people with dark skin, so they burn more easily. Tanned skin makes extra melanin to try to protect itself from the strong summer sun.

The sun's rays can badly harm a person's skin. In the summer, you should always wear sunscreen to protect your skin and a hat to shade your face and head.

Safe shade

The sun is hottest in the middle of the day, when it is high overhead. People in hot countries stay in the shade during the hottest hours. They know that the midday sun is dangerous because it is so strong.

Summer garden

In summer gardens, the sun's heat helps plants grow, flower, and make fruit.

Leaves at work

A green leaf uses sunshine to help it make food.

1. First, the leaf takes water from the ground and a gas called carbon dioxide from the air.

sunlight

2. The leaf uses sunlight and a green substance called chlorophyll to turn the water and carbon dioxide into sugary food and a gas called oxygen.

oxygen

carbon dioxide

3. The leaf uses the food to grow bigger and sends the oxygen out into the air. The way a leaf makes food for itself is called photosynthesis.

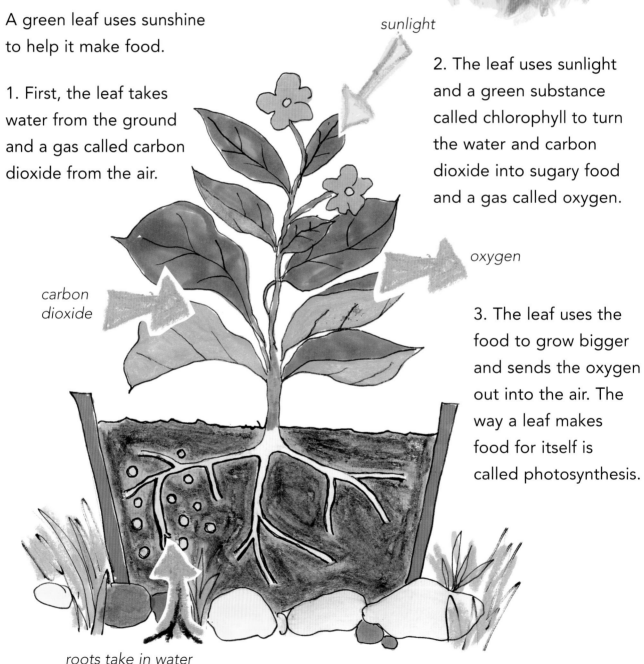

roots take in water

Summer smells

Flowers smell sweet to attract insects. They have bright colors, too. Some flowers even have lines and dots on them to guide insects to their nectar.

Flowers are for insects

In the summer, there are lots of insects to feed on the nectar deep inside each flower.

When an insect climbs into a flower, tiny pollen grains stick to its body. When it flies to another flower, it carries the pollen with it.

A flower needs pollen from a similar flower to fertilize it. Then it goes on to grow fruit and seeds.

Following the sun

The petals of many flowers open in sunshine and close at night. Some flowers even move to face the sun wherever it is in the sky. That way, they soak up as much sunshine as they can.

Sunflowers turn during the day to face the sun.

13

Summer farm

Farm crops and fruit grow and ripen in the sunshine.
A bowl of sweet summer fruit is delicious!

Crops for us

In the summer, you see fields of
cereal plants growing tall in the
sun. Wheat, oats, and barley are all
types of cereal. They are grown for
their seeds, called grain. We use
the grain to make food such as flour.

*Can you see the
grains of this wheat?
They are at the top.*

See the summer harvest

In late summer, crops are
ready to harvest. You might
see a big combine cutting the
cereal and separating the
grains from the stalks. In some
countries, farmers cut their
crops by hand with a long
knife called a scythe.

14

Tasty summer fruits

Once a flower has pollen from another flower, the summer sunshine helps it grow into a fruit. The fruit has seeds that might grow into a new plant.

Dried in sunshine

Some farmers grow crops that they dry in the sunshine to make food. Grapes are dried in the sun to make raisins. Tomatoes are dried in the sun to make them extra tasty.

Fruits to find

Fruits tempt animals to come and eat them. The animals carry away the fruit and help to spread the seeds to a new place. Soft fruit such as peaches, cherries, raspberries, and strawberries are all ripe and juicy in the summer.

The seed of a peach is inside the peach stone. It grows from a peach flower.

Summer animals

Summer is a busy time for animals.
There is a lot of food for them to gather.

Honey in the hive

Honeybees are busy in the summer. They live in groups, sometimes in man-made hives. The busiest bees are the worker bees. They make honey for baby bees (called larvae) to eat.

Every morning, worker bees leave the hive to look for nectar. When they find some, they take it to the hive, along with some pollen. They carry the pollen on their legs. The bees make nectar into honey and use pollen as food.

Sometimes you can see yellow pollen on the legs of worker bees.

Keeping cool

Humans are a kind of animal called a mammal. Mammals are animals with warm blood. Summer sunshine makes them even warmer. Some mammals, such as dogs, pant to cool down. The heat from their bodies comes out of their mouths. Some mammals, such as elephants, have very big ears. Lots of body heat comes out of them, like a radiator in a house.

Sunbathing reptiles

Reptiles love the warm sun. They do not have warm blood as mammals do. Instead, they need sunshine to warm them from outside and give them energy to move around. In the summer, reptiles like to bask in the sunshine.

Lizards, snakes, and crocodiles are all reptiles. They like to sunbathe.

Mammals like to stay in the shade when the sun is hot.

17

Hottest ever

The hottest summer places in the world are deserts.
They become very hot during the daytime.

Nightlife

Desert animals usually hide in the shade during the day. They might shelter under rocks or burrow into sand. Most animals come out at night, when the temperature drops. Reptiles and insects are the most common animals in deserts.

Hottest in the world

One of the world's hottest deserts is Death Valley, in California.

Camel power

Camels are good at living in the desert, even in the blistering heat of summer. They can go without food and water for many days. Their feet are wide so they can walk along easily in soft sand.

When rain never comes

A drought occurs when no rain falls for a long time during a longer and drier summer than normal. Water runs out, and the ground dries up. Plants die, and farmers lose their crops.

Drought can lead to famine. People and animals may starve when their food crops die.

A cloud of stinging sand

In sandy deserts, the summer heat can whip up sand and dust into a sandstorm that blocks out the sun.

If you were caught in a sandstorm, you would need to find shelter, or the blowing sand would sting your skin and get in your eyes and mouth.

Summer stories

All over the world, there are legends about the sun and summer. Here are some of them.

An Aborigine sun story

Good sky spirits make a fire in the sky every day. They collect firewood during the night and heap it up in the sky. Then they start the fire, and the blaze lights up Earth in the morning. By midday, the fire is at its fiercest and hottest. Then it dies away until a few red embers are left glowing in the evening.

An Inuit sun story

The Inuit people of Greenland have a sun goddess called Malina. She quarreled with her brother, the moon god, Anningan, smeared dirt over his face, and ran away across the sky. Her brother chases her but never catches her. That is why the sun, then the moon, appear above us.

A Chinese sun story

In Chinese legend, light and dark are always fighting. Sometimes dark gets the upper hand. Then Earth has longer nights. In the summer, light is winning the fight, so the days are longer.

A Japanese sun legend

Amaterasu is a Japanese sun goddess. She argued so much with her brother that she hid in a cave, and Earth was plunged into darkness. Then the other gods thought of a way to persuade her to come out. They held a party outside the cave entrance and placed a big mirror on a tree nearby. Hearing the party, Amaterasu peeked out and was so fascinated to see herself in the mirror that she came outside again, filling the world with light.

21

Summer parties

People celebrate summer with special parties.
Here are some of them.

Solstice parties

In northern lands, June 21st is the longest day of the year. It is called the summer solstice. In Finland, there are 23 hours of daylight, and everyone joins in a bonfire party called Johannus. They decorate their homes with flowers and birch branches.

In southern lands, December 21st is the summer solstice, the longest day. It's a good time to have parties and barbecues.

Sun festival

In Peru, June 24th marks Inti Raymi, the ancient Inca festival of the sun. It is still celebrated in the city of Cuzco, where the sun god is honored with music and dancing at the ancient sun temple.

Thanks for food

In Accra, a town in Ghana, Africa, the people of the Ga tribe celebrate their August harvest with the Homowo festival. Homowo means "making fun of hunger." It's a big party, with dancing and drumming, to thank the gods for the crops.

Summer dance

Traditionally, native North American tribes celebrate the summer corn harvest with a Green Corn Festival to thank the creator of the world for providing food. Sometimes they do a green corn celebration dance.

Paint the summer

Here are some ideas for making summery pictures.

Make your picture hot

Use warm colors to paint a summer picture. Try shades of yellow, red, and orange. They are the color of the sun and fire.

Put blue and yellow together to make a picture that looks full of sunlight.

Bright yellow next to bright blue in a picture makes the light look bright, just like in summer.

Summer shadows

When the sun shines brightly on things, they throw a shadow, so put some shadows in your summer pictures. Here are some rules to follow.

Sun lights up one side of an object but not the other. You can show this by adding some darker color.

Think about where the sunlight is coming from in your picture. A shadow falls on the ground away from the sun.

24

Paint a summer sunset

A good way to paint a warm, glowing sunset is to use wet paper, so the colors run together. You need thick white paper, masking tape, a glass of water, some poster paints, and brushes.

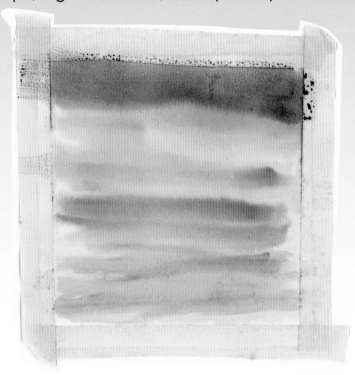

1. Tape the paper down flat on a table or board. Then paint all over it with clean water.

2. Paint watery yellow over the paper. Then paint watery red streaks across the yellow. The paints will run together.

3. Put a line of darker watery blue along the top, then let your picture dry.

4. Paint the sun and add some ground at the bottom of your picture.

Another way to make a glowing sunset picture is to glue torn strips of yellow, orange, and red tissue paper across a page so they overlap each other.

Make a piece of summer

Make your own hat to keep off the sun or a pretty seed necklace.

Chinese summer hat

In China, some farmers wear cone-shaped hats while working in the fields. To make one, you need a big piece of stiff paper or thin cardboard, a ruler, a pencil, scissors, and tape.

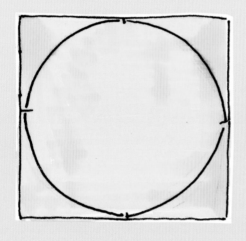

It doesn't matter if the circle isn't exactly right. You can trim it later.

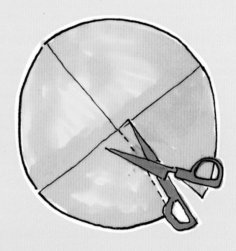

1. Draw a circle 20 inches (50 cm) wide by marking the middle point of each side, then joining the marks with curved lines.

2. Fold the circle in half, then in half again. Unfold it and cut along one of the folds to the middle.

3. Overlap the cut edges to make a shallow cone shape. Tape them underneath and then make sure the cone fits your head.

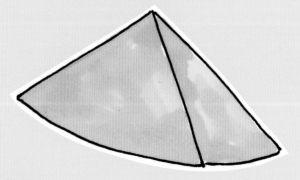

4. Decorate your hat with tissue, crepe paper, string, or paint. Tape on two ribbons to tie under your chin.

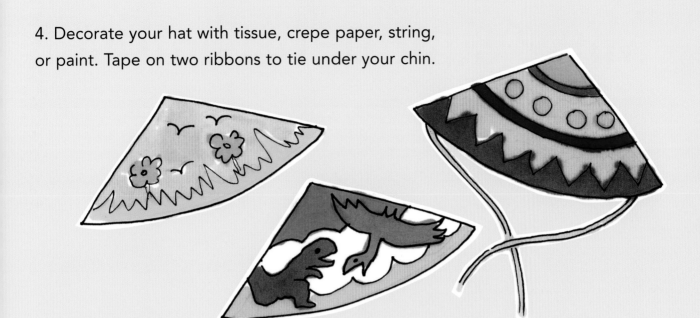

Fruit seed jewelry

You can make necklaces or bracelets from melon seeds. You need a tray, a thick needle, some thread, and an adult to help.

1. Scoop out the melon seeds and wash them. Put them on a tray and dry them in a warm cupboard or out in the sun.

2. Thread the needle and knot the end of the thread. Pierce each melon seed and pull the thread through it.

3. When you have finished, knot the ends of the thread tightly together.

Be a summer scientist

These summer experiments will help you discover the mystery of shadows and how much plants need sunlight.

Solve the shadow mystery

Do shadows change or stay the same? Make a cardboard shadow man to find the answer. You will need some cardboard, colored pencils, a sheet of white paper, some tape, and a compass, as well as a sunny day.

1. Draw and cut out a man shape from cardboard. Leave extra cardboard along the bottom to fold back so he stands up. Tape him to the white paper.

2. Early on a sunny morning, take the shadow man outside and stand him up facing south. Trace his shadow and write down the time.

3. Take the man outside again later and trace his shadow using a different color. Write down the time. Do this a third time later.

4. Look at the three tracings you have drawn. You will see that the shadow changes position and length during the day. Which is the shortest shadow?

Do plants need sunlight?

Find out whether plants need sunlight with two old, dry potatoes that are just beginning to sprout.

1. Put one potato in a dark cupboard, and the other potato on a sunny windowsill.

2. After a few days, look to see what is happening. Which has healthy green shoots, and which has weak, pale shoots?

The difference between the two potatoes is sunlight. It has helped the one on the windowsill grow healthy shoots.

Plants grow best when they are near sunlight.

Words to remember

crops Plants that farmers grow and harvest.

desert A place that is very dry. In the summer, deserts can be scorching hot.

drought A water shortage that happens if there is no rain for a long time.

equator The imaginary line around the middle of Earth.

evaporation Water disappearing into the air. The hot sun makes water evaporate.

hemispheres The northern and southern halves of Earth.

land of the midnight sun The far north of the world, where the sun shines day and night during the summer.

melanin A substance in your skin that helps to protect you from damaging rays of the sun.

nectar The sweet liquid inside a flower. Bees make honey from nectar.

photosynthesis A process that occurs when a green leaf collects water and a gas called carbon dioxide, then makes them into plant food and oxygen. To do this, the leaf needs sunlight and a green substance called chlorophyll.

pollen Tiny grains inside a flower. A flower needs pollen grains from a similar flower before it can grow fruit and seeds.

season A time of year that has a particular kind of weather and temperature.

summer solstice The longest day of the year. In the north, it is June 21st. In the south, it is December 21st.

temperature How hot or cold something is.

thermometer A tube with liquid inside that measures temperature.

Index